• Bartl

CAM

Streeuunder
MINI STREET ATLAS

CONTENTS

Legend 3
Key to Map Pages .... 4 - 5
City Centre Maps .... 6 - 9
Map Pages .... 10 - 22
Places of Interest .... 23 - 24
Index to Street Names .... 25 - 35

Bartholomew
A Division of HarperCollins*Publishers*

ISBN 0 7028 1852 6
E/B 5523 ENU

Printed in Great Britain by Bartholomew,
HarperCollins Manufacturing, Edinburgh.

Legend, Légende, Zeichenerklärung

Main through road
axe principal, Durchgangsstraße

Secondary road
axe secondaire, Verbindungsstraße

Other road
autre rue, sonstige Straße

Railway
ligne ferroviaire, Eisenbahn

Built-up area
noyau urbain, bebautes Gebiet

Recreation area
terrain de sport, Sportgelände

Church
église, Kirche

Police station
poste de police, Polizeiwache

Post office
bureau de poste, Postamt

School
école, Schule

Car park
parking, Parkplatz

One-way street
sens unique, Einbahnstraße

Pedestrian precinct
zone pour piétons, Fußgängerzone

Closed to traffic
circulation interdite, Verkehr verboten

Roundabout
rond-point, Kreisverkehr

Scale 1: 12 500 (5 inches to 1 mile)

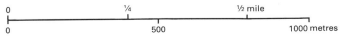

4

KEY TO MAP PAGES

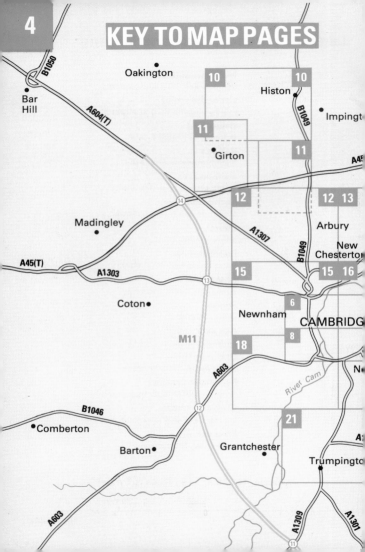

Oakington

B1050

Bar Hill

A604(T)

Histon

10 10

B1049

Impingto

11

11

Girton

A45

12

Madingley

14

A1307

B1049

Arbury

A45(T)

A1303

13

15

New Chesterton

12 13

15 16

Coton

6

Newnham

CAMBRIDG

M11

8

18

A603

River Cam

N

21

B1046

Comberton

12

Barton

Grantchester

Trumpington

A603

A1309

A1301

11

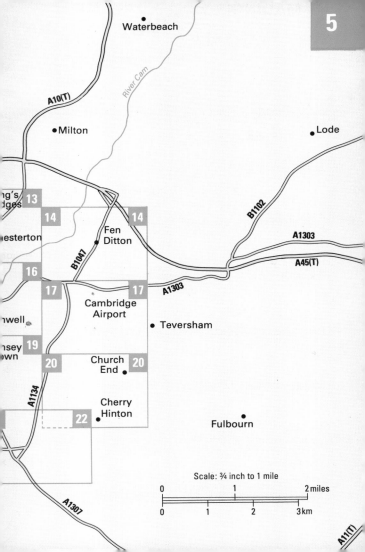

Waterbeach

River Cam

A10(T)

Milton

Lode

ng's
dges **13**

14   **14**

esterton   Fen
                  Ditton   B1102

                                  A1303

                  B1047   A45(T)

16

17   **17** A1303

                  Cambridge
                  Airport

nwell   Teversham

sey **19**
own

20   Church **20**
                End

A1134

                  Cherry
                  Hinton
            22

                        Fulbourn

Scale: ¾ inch to 1 mile

0   1   2 miles

0   1   2   3km

A1307

A11(T)

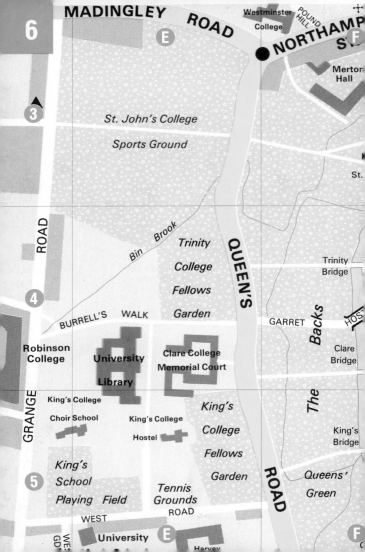

6

MADINGLEY ROAD

E

Westminster College

POUND HILL

NORTHAMP ST

F

Merton Hall

St. John's College
Sports Ground

St.

ROAD

Bin Brook

Trinity
College
Fellows
Garden

QUEEN'S

Trinity Bridge

4

BURRELL'S WALK

GARRET

The Backs

HOS

Robinson College

University
Library

Clare College
Memorial Court

Clare Bridge

King's College
Choir School

King's College
Hostel

King's
College
Fellows
Garden

The

King's Bridge

GRANGE

King's
School
Playing Field

Tennis
Grounds
ROAD

ROAD

Queens'
Green

5

WEST

WEST GD

University

E

Harvey

F

Magdalene
College

MAGDALENE ST.

QUAYSIDE LANE

ST. JOHN'S RD.

THOMPSON'S LANE

NEW PORTUGAL PL.

NEW PK. ST.

LOWER PARK ST.

PARK PARADE

G

A

3

BRIDGE STREET

Court

ohn's

College

ighs

idge

ST. JOHN'S ST.

Holy
Sepulchre

ROUND
CHURCH
ST.

PARK STREET

P

Wesley House

JESUS

MALCOLM ST.

Westcott
House

LAN

KING

MANG

Trinity

College

ALL SAINT'S
PASSAGE

Blue Boar
Hotel

SIDNEY

Sidney
Sussex
College

TRINITY LANE

Gonville &
Caius
College

SENATE HOUSE PASSAGE

Old
Schools

Senate
House

LANE

TRINITY STREET

KINGS PARADE

ST. JOHN'S ST.

GIFFORD PL.

GREEN

ROSE CRES.

ST.
MARY'S
ST.

Great
St.
Mary's

Chapel

King's

College

re
ge

STREET

MARKET ST.

MARKET PASSAGE

MARKET

SUSSEX ST.

HOBSON'S
PASSAGE

County
Hall

HOBSON STREET

**Christ's
College**

4

MILTON'S

First
Court

CHRIST'S LA.

DRUMM

STREET

ST ANDREW'S

PETTY CURY

Lion Yard
Shopping Centre

POST OFFICE
TERR.

North
Court

EMMAN

Arts
Theatre

Guildhall

i

BENE'T ST.

WHEELER

ST.
PARSON'S
CT.

GUILDHALL ST.

◆ Library

CORN EXCHANGE ST.

P

ST. TIBB'S ROW

H.P.O.

PEAS HILL

St. Bene'ts

FREE SCHOOL LANE

KING'S LA.

Zoology
Museum

Whipple
Museum

QUEENS'
LANE

eens'
lege

St.
Catherine's
College

Corpus
Christi
College

G

BOTOLPH LA.

EMBROKE ST.

DOWNING

STREET

Sedgwick
Museum

Museum of
O ogy

Museum of
A h l

DOWNING

Cannon
Cinema

5

P

EET

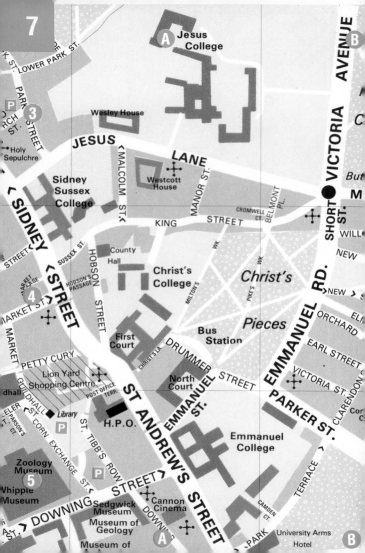

INSET SCALE 1:6250

7

100   200   C   300   440yds   D

100   200   300   400 metres

TREE AV.

ABETH WAY

mmer

on

NORTH TERRACE

BRUNSWICK WK.

BRUNSWICK GDNS.

BRUNSWICK TERR.

PARSONAGE ST.

AUCKLAND RD.

BAILEY MS.

3

CAUSEWAY

FAIR STREET

SALMON LA.

WILLOW PL.

FAIR CT.

CAUSEWAY PASSAGE

JAMES ST.

CHRIST CHURCH ST.

NAPIER ST.

NEWMARKET RD.

SUN ST.

WELLINGTON ST.

WELLINGTON PASSAGE

SEVERN PL.

PARKER TERR.

NEW STREET

FITZROY LANE

P

P

NELSON CLO.

NELSON ST.

CRISPIN PL.

ST. MATTHEW'S

YOUNG ST.

P

4

FITZROY ST.

Grafton Centre

P

SQUARE

PORTLAND PL.

EDEN ST.

REEDEN ST. BACKWAY

CITY ROAD

BURLEIGH ROAD

PARADISE ST.

GRAFTON ST.

BURLEIGH PLACE

BURLEIGH STREET

STREET

STAFFORDSHIRE STREET

ROAD

SMART'S ROW

STREET

JOHN STREET

BRANDON PL.

DOVER ST.

ADAM

NORFOLK STREET

CAROLINE PL.

FLOWER ST.

BLOSSOM ST.

NORFOLK TERRACE

STREET

STREET

PROSPECT ROW

WARKWORTH ST.

EAST

BROAD STREET

WARKWORTH TERR.

Police Sta.

BRADMORE STREET

College

Theatre

5

Fire Sta.

PARKSIDE

BRADMORE LA.

PALMERS WK.

Peter's Field

G.P.O.

Sorting

College of Art &

Tec **D** **logy**

C

D

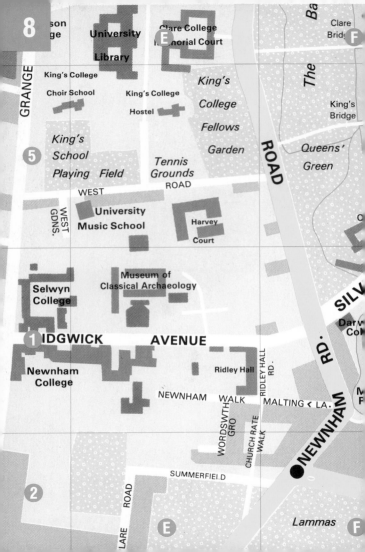

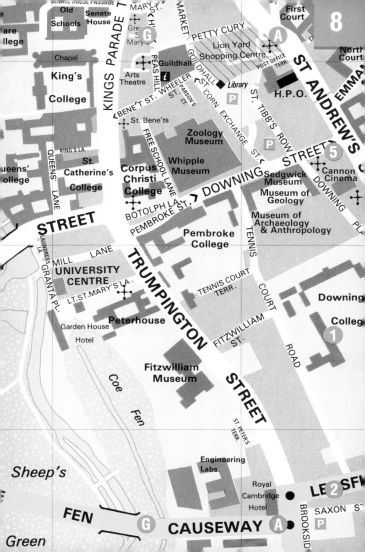

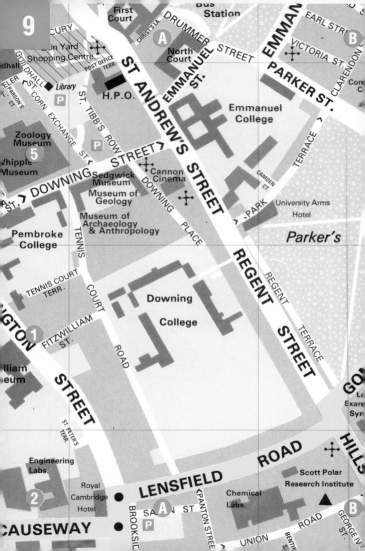

D   E   F   GLEBE ROAD   G

GUN'S LANE

COTTENHAM

B1049

PARLOUR CLO.
ALICE WAY
PEACOCK WAY

BARROWCROFTS RD.

CROFT CLO.

ALSTEAD RD.

NORMANTON WAY
GREENLEAS

FARMSTEAD CLO.

OSIER'S WAY

BURY WAY

DT3

NARROW CLO.

GARDEN WALK

YOUNGMAN AV.

YOUNG MAN CLO.

Abbey Farm

COTTENHAM RD.

ST ANDREW'S PARK

WINDERS LANE

IVINS ORCHARD

OLD CLAY STREET

OLD FARM CLO.

ALLINGTON CLO.

TUCKETTS CLO.

ORCHARD RD.

CHURCH ST.

KINGSWAY

SYMONDS CLO.

NARROW LANE

SPRING CLO.

MILL LANE

PADDOCK CLO.

LANE

PARK

BELL HILL

HARDING WAY

LANE

WINDMILL LA.

SCHOOL HOUSE HILL

PRIOR'S CLO.

WAY

Playing   Field

PARK AV.

AINGERS RD.

SHIRLEY RD.

MERTON RD.

P   HISTON
   P.O.

THE GREEN

HIGH ST.

1

2

3

4

5

PARK

SOMERSET RD.

HOME CLOSE

WYER-JOYCE CLO.

WEST RD.

STATION

WATER   LANE

IMPINGTON   LANE

HEREWARD CLOSE

BISHOP WAY

ROAD

SAFFRON RD.

HEREFORD CLO.

ROSE HOMEFIELD RD.

THE COLE

NEW SCHOOL ROAD

NEW SCHOOL RD.

POPLAR RD.

SCHOOL LA.

DANEY CLO.

STARR CLO.

HENRY CLO.

MORRIS

ROAD

BRACKENBURY

Elec. Sub.
Station

LOVE'S CLO.

KAY HITCH WAY

MACFARLANE RD.

NEW

MOWLAM CLO.

CHIVERS   WAY

CHEQUERS RD.

D   E   11   F   Vision Park   G   BRI

P.O.

Recreation

A Girton Farm

B

10

C

Golf rse **1**

FAIRWAY

NORTHFIELD RD.

DODFORD LANE

Manor Farm

2

COCKERTON RD.

School

STREET

HIGH

WOODLANDS PK.

3

Gretton Ct

THE GOWERS

MICHAELS CLO.

NASHPIT RD.

DUCK END

CHURCH LANE

HICK'S LANE

LEES WAY

CAMBRIDGE

GIRTON

MARK'S WAY

ORCHARD CLO.

RED GATE

P.O.

STERNDALE CLO.

RD.

4

CHERRY BOUNDS RD.

ROAD

P.S.

MAYFIELD RD.

WOODY GREEN

ST. VINCENT'S

GIFFORD'S CLO.

CLOSE

PEPYS WAY

5

A { Girton

B { WELLBROOK CT. **12**

C

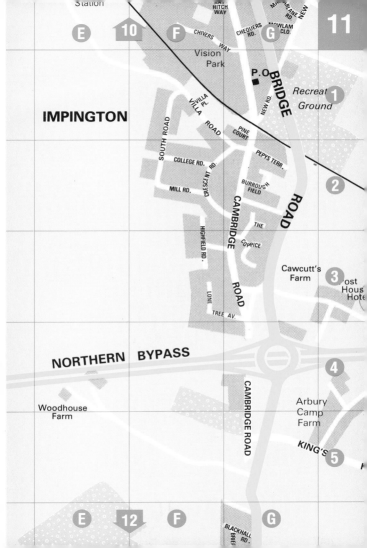

Station

HITCH WAY

CHIVERS WAY

CHEQUERS RD.

MOWLAM CLO.

MACFARLANE NEW

NEW

Vision Park

P.O.

BRIDGE

New RD.

Recreat Ground 1

IMPINGTON

VILLA PL.

VILLA ROAD

SOUTH ROAD

PINE COURT

PEPYS TERR.

COLLEGE RD.

CRESCENT RD.

BURROUGH FIELD

MILL RD.

CAMBRIDGE

ROAD

2

THE COPPICE

HIGHFIELD RD.

Cawcutt's Farm

3

ost Hous Hote

LONE

TREE AV.

NORTHERN BYPASS

CAMBRIDGE ROAD

4

Woodhouse Farm

Arbury Camp Farm

KING'S 5

BLACKHALL BRIEF

A **B** **C** **D**

KINGS

HED

1

ROAD

ST. ALBANS ROAD

JERMYN

CLOSE

CALLANDER CLO.

JOHN BUCHAN RD.

BANFF SOMERL MITCHELL

MONTR CLO.

NEPTUNE WAY

NORTHFIELD

CAMERON ROAD

NUNS WAY

MOYNE CLO.

ASHVALE

ABBOTS CL.

ALBEMARLE RD.

ARAGON CL.

CRATHERN WAY

CADWIN FIELD

CROWLAND WAY

AYLESBOROUGH CLO.

VERULAM WAY

SOMERSET CL.

ELLESMERE RD.

ARBURY

SACKVILLE CL.

WOBURN CL.

ROXBURGH RD.

ENNISDALE RD.

NORTHFIELD

CROWLAND

WAY

WHITFIELD

CAMPKIN

HAWKINS RD.

HAVILAND WAY

FORDWICH CLO.

NORTH CL.

BRACKLEY CL.

ROAD

MONTROSE CL.

WINDLESHAM

WAX

FIELD

NICHOLSON

CLO.

WAY

2

TLAND

ARBURY

BUTTER WAY

WAY

HUMPHREYS RD.

FORTESCUE ROAD

MONTGO

WAY

P

ALEX WOOD RD.

MANSEL WAY

Library

MERE WAY

ARBURY ROAD

12

RS

WAY

TOPHAM WAY

COCKE

HAY FARM RD.

CARLTON WAY

WAVELL CL.

CUNNINGHAM CL.

CL.

Magdalene C

Sports Gro

WARD RD.

PERSE WAY

3

BRIMLEY ROAD

ESSEX

RD

ROLAND CL.

CL.

DUNNING

MONTGOMERY RD.

WAY

REDFERN

HIGHFIELD AV.

LEYS AV.

HAVENFIELD

CL.

4

BERT ROAD

METCALFE ROAD

COURTNEY WAY

HURST

PARK

ORCHARD AV.

LEYS ROAD

MULBERRY CL.

MARFIELD CT.

KIRKBY

RO

OAK TREE AV.

BATESON RD.

AV.

HIGHWORTH AV.

MAPLE CL.

5

GARDEN WALK

P

New Chesterton

GURNEY RD.

ASCHAM RD.

ATHERTON CLO.

Lib.

MILTON

CHESTERTON HALL CR.

CHESTNUT GROVE

WAY

HAWTHORN

LABURNUM CLO.

EL

AB

VICTORIA PARK

PRIMROSE ST.

GREEN'S RD.

A

Cambridge City Football Club

SPRING

HERBERT STREET

B

SPRINGF RD.

GEORGE ST

16

CHA CL.

C

ROAD

ANDY LA

MILTON

14

A **B** **C** **D**

NUFFIEL

▲

1

CAM L

13

LANE

Lomas
Farm

Long Reach
House

Hall
Farm

GROVE

BOURNE ROAD

CHETNEY

FAIRBAIRN CL

LONG REACH RD.

MOSS BANK

FEN ROAD

AN L

IZAAK WALTON WAY

LENT'S WAY

WAY

MAY'S WAY

FALLOW-FIELD

WAY

2

P

3

River   Cam

Common

4

HOW

MANN'S RD.

16

ROAD

5

RONALD
ROLPH
CT.

WALK

DITTON FIELDS

DITTON

FERNDALE
RISE

FIELDS

DITTON

DITTON

DITTON

FIELDS

FIELDS

HOWARD
CL.

HEADFORD
CL.

WADLOES

ROAD

HOWARD RD.

HOWARD ROAD

EGERTON CL.

EG.
RD

DUDLEY

RD.

KEYNES RD.

EKIN

RD.

HUN

WADLOES

HOWARD RD.

▲

■ P.O.

●

ELFLEDA RD.

QUANTON CLO.

Cambridge United
Football Club

A

STANES-
FIELD CLO.

STANESFIELD RD.

B

RAWLYN CL.

NO L CL.

17

WHITE

C

Lib.

⊹

GREEN END

WRIGHT'S CLO.

FIELD LANE (Track)

NEWMARK

A45

1

CHURCH

FEN

DITTON

BAKERY CLO.

HIGH

MUSGRAVE WAY

P.S.

2

STREET

P.O.

Home Farm

HIGH DITCH ST.

3

LANE

SMORE CL.

FISON RD.

TIPTREE CLO.

RACHEL CLO.

ANN'S RD.

LEONARD CLO.

HELEN CLO.

VELOS WK.

DENNIS RD.

BERG HOLT

COGGESHALL CLO.

CHIG. WELL CT.

THE RODINGS

BRENTWOOD CLO.

THORPE WAY

4

lth tre

tery

Greenhouse Farm

5

NEWMARKET

MEADOW-LANDS RD.

HOMIN

17

ROAD

NEWMARK

A1303

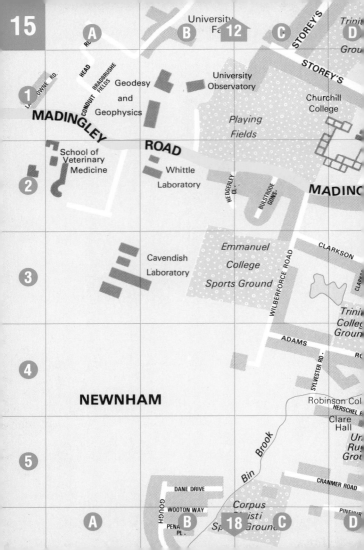

A

B

University
Fa

12

C

STOREY'S

D

Trini

Grou

STOREY'S

RU

HEAD

BRADRUSHE
FIELDS

CONDUIT

1

LA ... OWNE RD.

Geodesy
and
Geophysics

University
Observatory

Churchill
College

Playing
Fields

MADINGLEY

ROAD

School of
Veterinary
Medicine

Whittle
Laboratory

HEDGERLEY
CL.

BULSTRODE
GDNS.

MADINGTO

2

Cavendish
Laboratory

Emmanuel
College

Sports Ground

CLARKSON

WILBERFORCE ROAD

CLARK

3

Trini

Colleg

Groun

ADAMS

RO

4

NEWNHAM

SYLVESTER RD.

Robinson Col

HERSCHEL

Clare
Hall

Ur

Ru

Gro

5

Bin

Brook

CRANMER ROAD

DANE DRIVE

GOUGH

WOOTON WAY

PENA

PL.

Corpus

...isti

Sp... Ground

18

PINEWI

A

B

C

D

DON

CANTER-
BURY
HALIF...
ST.
CHRIS... ST.
ST. STEPHEN'S PL.
WEST... AV.

PRIORYFIELD

WESTFIELD

BENSON

LA.

BEN...

NORTH

ST.

BERMUDA RD.
BERMUDA TERR.

FRENCH...

HARVEY GOO...

STRETTON

GARDEN WAL...

VICTORIA

C...

ARTHUR ST.
CAPTHUR ST.
CLARE HALE ST.
ST. LUKE'S ST.

HILDA ST.

SEARLE ST.
CARLYLE ST.

PRIMROSE ST.
FISHER ST.
VICTORIA PARK
HOLLAND ST.
GREEN'S ST.

P.O.

ROAD

1

william
llege

ROAD

New
Hall

P Castle
Court

ALPHA
HERTFORD
ST.

ALBERT ST.

GRASMERE
GDNS.
ROAD

C

St.
Edmund's

BUCKINGHAM RD.

CASTLE **P.S.**

MAGRATH AV.

EAST
HERT.
ST.

Jes

SHELLEY ROW
MT.
PLEASANT
MOUNT

Shire
Hall

Castle
Mound

2

Lucy
Cavendish
College

MARGARET RD.
LADY

ALBION
ROW
SHER.
GDN
CASTLE
ROW

CASTLE
ST.

CHESTERTON
LANE

ROAD

ST.
PETERS
ST.

WHY...

KING...
HONEY
HILL
HAY...

P.O.

MAGDALENE

16

OAD

COLKCROFT
PL.

NORTHAMPTON
ST.

BRIDGE

3

ST.

JESUS

St. John's College

QUEEN'S

JOHN'S
ST.
TRINITY
ST.

NO...

Te

Trinity
College

ST.

4

University
Library

ROAD

The
Backs

King's
College

KING'S PARADE

MARKET
ST.

SIDNEY ST.

ST.

ROAD

GRANGE

WEST
GDNS.

WEST ROAD

5

DOWNIN
ST.

PEMBROKE
ST.

Selwyn
llege

SIDGWICK

AVENUE

TENNIS

JIMP...

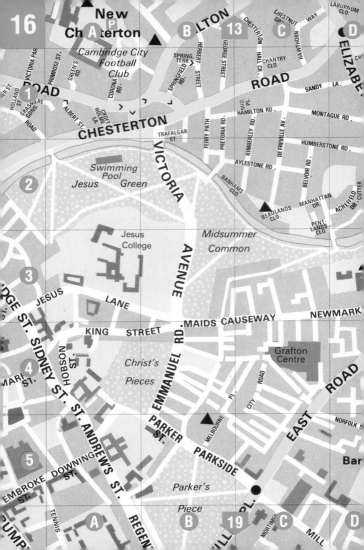

New
Ch♠terton

A P

B ILTON **13** **C**

D ELIZABE

Cambridge City
Football
Club

CHESTNUT GR

CHESTERTON HALL CR.

HAWTHORN WAY

LABURNUM CLO.

SPRING TERR.

SPRINGFIELD RD.

HERBERT STREET

GEORGE STREET

CHANTRY CLO.

1 ROAD

HOLLAND ST.

VICTORIA PARK

PRIMROSE ST.

GREEN'S RD.

GRASMERE GDNS.

CORONA

CROFT HOLME LA.

ALBERT ST.

ROAD

ROAD

SANDY LA.

MONTAGUE RD.

CHESTERTON

TRAFALGAR ST.

FERRY PATH

PRETORIA RD.

HAMILTON RD.

KIMBERLEY RD.

DE FREVILLE AV.

AYLESTONE RD.

HUMBERSTONE RD.

2 Swimming
Pool

Jesus Green

VICTORIA

BANHAMS CLO.

BELVOIR RD.

MANHATTAN DR.

ACREFIELD DR.

CUTTER

BEADLANDS CLO.

PENT-LANDS CLO.

3 Jesus
College

Midsummer
Common

AVENUE

JESUS LANE

KING STREET

MAIDS CAUSEWAY

NEWMARK

Grafton
Centre

Christ's
Pieces

EMMANUEL RD.

PL.

CITY ROAD

EAST ROAD

4 SIDNEY ST.

MARI ST.

HOBSON ST.

ST.

NORFOLK

5 EMBROKE ST.

DOWNING ST.

ST. ANDREW'S ST.

PARKER ST.

MELBOURNE

PARKSIDE

Bar

Parker's
Piece

TENNIS

A **B** **19** **C**

REGENT

PL.

MORTIMER RD

MILL

UMP♦

erton
pital

D

P

P.O.

CHAPEL ST.

WALT.

E

13

WATER ST.

FERRY LA.

F

G

Stourbridge Comm

CHURCH ST.

CHURCH ST.

CAMSIDE

LYNFIELD LA.

ecreation
Ground

1

ST. ANDREW'S RD.

Playing
Field

STANLEY

REGATTA
CT.

ROW

OYSTER

MERCER'S

SWANN'S RD.

ROW

14

MARINER'S
WAY

LOGAN'S
WAY

ROAD

GARLIC
ROW

2

CAPSTAN
CLO.

Museum
of
Technology

NEWMARKET

ROAD

Cambridge

RIVERSIDE

THE
MALLARDS

CHEDDARS LA.

Football

ABBEY RD.

PRIORY RD.

SAXON RD.

BECHE ROAD

GODSTONE
RD.

RIVER LANE

3

P.O.

HENLEY RD.

COLDHAM'S ROAD

OCCUPATION
RD.

ABBEY ST.

HARVEST WAY

STREET

Coldh

NEW

SILVERWOOD
CLO.

COLDHAM'S

4

JUNG ST.

PETWORTH
ST.

GELDART
ST.

ABBEY WK.

ABBEY WK.

YORK STREET

ROAD

C

17

VICARAGE
TERR.

EDWARD
ST.

STREET

YORK TERR.

CROMWELL

ROAD

BRAMPTON

ROAD

STOURBRIDGE

LANE

5

STREET

GWYD

STURTON

SLEAFORD ST.

AINS-
WORTH
CT.

STONE ST.

AINS-
WORTH

ROSS ST.

VINERY
RD.

D

E

23

F

FAIRFAX

ROAD

G

VINERY RD.

GWYDIR

KERR-
IDGE
CLO.

HOOPER ST.

D   E   14   F   G   Greenh
Farm

NEWMARKET

NEWMARKET   ROAD

A1303

1

HOMING

THETFORD TER.
MEADOW-LANDS RD.

ort Terminal

2

CHUR
3 R
Teversha

CAMBRIDGE

AIRPORT

4

5

D
ENE CL.
SEMARY LA.   E   20   RCH   F   G   ROAD
LA.

A

Bin

CRANMER

B 15 **C** **D**

DRIVE

GOUGH

WOOTON WAY

PENARTH
PL.

Corpus
Christi
Sports Ground

PINEHU

WAY

SPENS
AV.

Wolfson
College

SELWYN (

STUKELEY
CL.

PEARCE
CLO.

1

BARTON CL.

BARTO

King's and
Selwyn College
Sports Ground

Queen's
Sports
Ground

BYZWAY

2

FULBROOKE RD.

SELWYN RD.

KING'S RO

Cambridge
Rugby
Football Ground

Trinity New
Field

Pembroke
Sports
Ground

3

ROAD

4

GRANTCHESTER

5

A **B** **C** River **D**

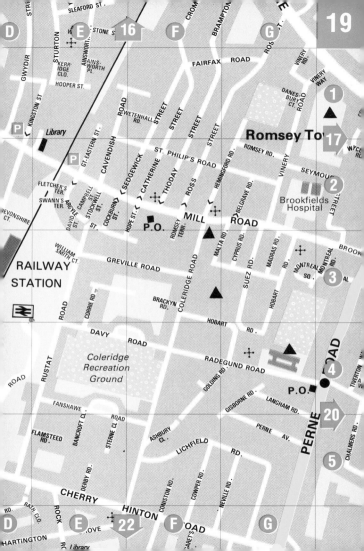

D · E · 16 · F · G

STREET
SLEAFORD ST.
STONE S
CROM
BRAMPTON

STURTON
KERRIDGE CLO.
AINSWORTH PL
AINSWORTH
FAIRFAX ROAD
ROS
VINERY
WAY

HOOPER ST.
GWYDIR

KINGSTON ST.
ROAD
DANESBURY CT.
VINERY ROAD

1

P
Library
GT. EASTERN ST.
CAVENDISH
WETENHALL RD.
STREET
STREET
STREET
STREET
ROMSEY RD.
VINERY
Romsey To
17
WYC

P
FLETCHER'S TER.
CAMPBELL
SEDGEWICK
CATHERINE
ST. PHILIP'S ROAD
THODAY
ROSS
HEMINGFORD RD.
SEYMOU
2

DEVONSHIRE CT.
SWANN'S TER.
ARGYLE
STOCKWELL ST.
DAVID ST.
COCKBURN ST.
HOPE ST.
ROMSEY TER.
MILL
BELGRAVE RD.
Brookfields Hospital

WILLIAM SMITH CT.
P.O.
ROAD
MALTA RD.
CYPRUS RD.
MADRAS RD.
MONTREAL
BROOK

RAILWAY
STATION
GREVILLE ROAD
COLERIDGE ROAD
SUEZ RD.
RD.
MONTREAL SQ.
3
AL

CORRIE RD.
ROAD
BRACKYN RD.
HOBART
HOBART RD.

DAVY ROAD
RADEGUND ROAD
ROAD
4
TIVERTO

Coleridge
Recreation
Ground
GOLDING RD.
P.O.

ROAD
FANSHAWE
RUSTAT
BANCROFT CL.
STERNE CL.
ROAD
ASHBURY CL.
GISBORNE RD.
LANGHAM RD.
PERNE
PERNE
20

FLAMSTEED RD.
DERBY RD.
LICHFIELD
RD.
PERNE AV.
CHALMERS RD.
5

CHERRY
RATH CLO.
ROCK
CONISTON RD.
COWPER RD.
NEVILLE RD.
HINTON

RD.
HARTINGTON
GROVE
22
Library
ROAD

D · E · F · G

ROSEMARY LA.

NE CL.

CHURCH

END

MARCH

LANE

MARCH
LANE

TEVERSHAM DRIFT

Church End

CHERRY HINTON ROAD

GAZELLE WAY

CARIBOU
WAY

IMPALA DR.

DOLPHIN CLO.

PAN
WAY

BUFFALO
WAY

ANTELOPE WAY

MANDRILL
CLO.

THE
LYNX

LEMUR
DR.

LORIS
CT.

GAZELLE WAY

FENNEC
CLO.

1

2

WOLSEY WAY

IVER WAY

NEWELL
WK.
CLO.

QUEEN'S
MEADOW

NEALE
CL.

ORCHARD ESTATE

ST. ANDREW'S
GLEBE

DRIFT

TEVERSHAM

KELSEY
CLO.

SABLE
CLO.

LEYBURN
CLO.

PROVIN-
BOURNE
CLO.

ROEDEER
CLO.

TAMARIN
GDNS.

3

STER RD.

G/CT. RD.

CROWTHORNE

CLAYGATE RD.

CHARTFIELD RD.

CHAL-
FONT
CLO.

CHELWOOD RD.

ESMOND AV.

LOVE LA.

MILL END
CLO.

P.O.

GLADSTONE WAY

HEADINGTON
CLO.

HEADINGTON DR.

FERNLEA CL.

PAMPLIN
CT.

RAILWAY ST.

HIGH STREET

LANG-
DALE
CLO.

TENBY
CL.

WINDER
MERE
CLO.

FULBOURN

BURNHAM
CLO.

BLISS
WAY

HIGHDENE

WELSTEAD
RD.

SUNMEAD
WK.

LISLE
WK.

RUSH
GRO.

OLD

DRIFT

Cherry Hinton

HIGH
ST.

FISHER'S

WENYDE
CLO.

ARBAN
CLO.

AUGERS
RD.

PEN CL.

COLVILLE

ROAD

LANE

SHEPHERD'S
CL.

LEETE ROAD

KEATES ROAD

DRAYTON
CLO.

DRAYTON RD.

MALLETS RD.

BRIDEWELL RD.

LUCERNE CLO.

SPEEDWELL
CLO.

VALERIAN
CT.

VIOLET
CLO.

TEASEL
CLO.

CLOVER
CT.

COMFREY
CT.

HAREBELL
CLO.

YARROW
WAY

COLTSFOOT CLO.

4

P

■ Library

*Recreation
Ground*

5

Fulbourn
Hospital

FULBOURN ROAD

AINSDALE TWEEDALE

CAMBRIDGE ROAD

D E F G

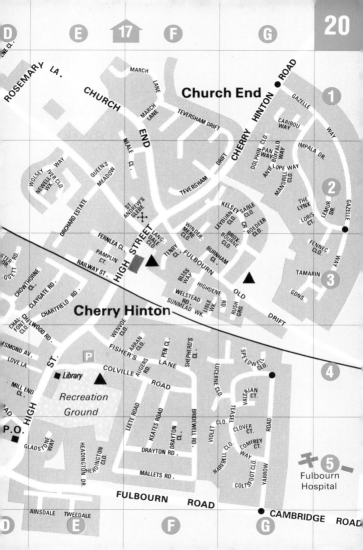

A   B   **18**   C   D

River

1

2

3

NORTH COTTS

LO

GAZELEY RD.

WAY

WINGATE   WINGATE CLO.

4

STREET

ALPHA TERR.

Trumpington Hall

WINCHMOR DR.

P.O

SEFTON CLO.

LAMB. CLO.

SOUTH CLO.

HIGH

SCOTS DOWNE RD

MONKSWELL

GAYT. CLO.

5

CAMPBELL LANE

CHURCH LA.

BEVERLY WAY

LINGREY CT.

PAGET

ROAD

GRANTCHESTER   ROAD

MARIS LA.

ANSTEY WAY

BYRON

ROAD

ANSTEY WAY

A   B   C

SQU

Hospital

Government
Buildings

19

HOMERTON
ST.

P.C.

St. Faith's
School

NEWTON ROAD

RAYLEIGH
CLO.

BENTLEY ROAD

DIAMOND CLO.

Cambridge Univ.

Press

PURBECK RD.

CORFE
CLO.

HILLS

RA

1

Homerton
College

BARROW ROAD

BARROW CLO.

Clare College
Playing
Fields

ORSON ROAD

WAINS
WT.
CT.

Prep
ol

BARROW RD.

Sports
Ground

RUTHERFORD RD.

LUARD

LUARD CL.

ROAD

2

SEDLEY TAYLOR RD.

Playing
Field

22

3

The Pea

ROAD

LON

pington

Cambridgeshire
High Sch. for Girls

4

ROBINSON WAY

5

A brook

Hospital

and

Medical Sch

A

B

19

C

D

PURBECK RD.

CORPE CLO.

ELSWORTH PL.

CHERRY

HINTON

ROAD

NEVILLE RD.

COWPER RD.

CONIST.

RATHMORE RD.

RATH CLO.

ROCK

GROVE

HILLS

HARTINGTON

MARSHALL RD.

ROAD

Library

GROVE

MAGNOLIA CLO.

ST. MARGARET'S SQ.

1

Homerton College

BLINCO

AVENUE

AV.

LADY JANE CT.

CAVENDISH

BALDOCK WAY

HINTON

COURTLAND AV.

ROAD

LUARD CL.

2

EDNDALE CLO.

AVENUE

21

HILLS

ALLIANCE CT.

ROAD

SEDLEY TAYLOR RD.

GLEBE

MOWBRAY

3

The Perse School

HOLBROOK ROAD

DEAN DR.

LONG

ROAD

QU. EDITH'S WAY

QUEE

FENDON CL.

FENDON

ROAD

4

eshire or Girls

Recreation Ground

NIGHTINGALE

ROBINSON WAY

ROTHERWICK WAY

TO

5

Addenbrooke's

Hospital

and

STANSGATE AV.

RED CROSS LANE

GREENLANDS

FI

Medical School

A

B

C

D

PLACES OF INTEREST

COLLEGES

Christ's   7 A4
Founded in 1505, in St. Andrew's Street and adjoining Christ's Piece, open ground flanked by Milton's Walk which is named after John Milton, who was entered here.

Churchill   15 C1
Founded 1960 and inspired by Sir Winston Churchill's wish to forward scientific and technological studies.

Clare   6 F4
Backing onto the river, best approached via Trinity Lane this College was founded 1326, destroyed by fire and refounded in 1338 by Lady Elizabeth de Clare. Another fire destroyed the medieval buildings. The present courtyard dates from 1638.

Corpus Christi   8 G5
Founded 1352, situated in Pembroke Street and noted for its charming 'Old Court' to the north of main building.

Downing   9 A1
Founded 1800 is in Regent Street, opposite Parker's Piece. At Cavendish Lab. in Downing Street, behind the College, Rutherford made his famous experiments in the structure of atoms.

Emmanuel   7 A5
Founded in 1584 by Sir Walter Mildmay. John Harvard, founder of the American University of that name studied here. It is in St. Andrew's Street. There is a notable Wren Chapel.

Fitzwilliam   15 D1
Founded 1966 to provide for non-collegiate students in the houses near the Fitzwilliam Museum. The building was the work of Denys Lasdun.

Gonville and Caius   6 G4
Founded 1348 and situated between Trinity Lane and Trinity Street backing on to river Cam. The 'Honour and Virtue' gates of Caius are famous.

Homerton   21 G1
Established in Cambridge in 1894 as a teacher training college, Homerton became part of the University in 1978 when a degree course in Education was introduced for all students.

Jesus   7 A3
Founded 1496 by Bishop Alcock of Ely. Situated between Jesus Lane and Jesus Green. The College was developed from the buildings of a former Benedictine nunnery and retains the former Chapel. The attractive main gates were part of the Bishop of Ely's design for the college.

King's   8 G5
Founded 1441 is in King's Parade, but backs onto the Cam. The view from the 'Backs' is superb. Its chief glory is the Chapel with its fan-vaulted roof of unsurpassed magnificence. The glass in the Chapel is the most complete and largest series of ancient windows in the world.

Magdalene   6 G32
Founded in 1542 and situated in Magdalene Street across Magdalene Bridge. Lord Audley of Walden endowed the College with some of his spoils from the Dissolution of the Monasteries. It has two charming little Courts and a shady garden.

New Hall   15 E1
Founded 1954, this is a college for ladies, situated on the Huntingdon Road.

Newnham   8 D1
Founded in 1871 this too is a ladies College situated in Sidgwick Avenue and a further triumph for would-be women graduates two years after the foundation of Girton.

Pembroke   8 G5
Founded 1347 by Mary de Valence, Countess of Pembroke, the College is situated between Trumpington Street, Pembroke Street and Tennis Court Road. The famous Chapel was the first building designed by Christopher Wren. Noted for its clerics and poets among former scholars, but was also the College of 'Young Mr. Pitt'. Attractive Fellows Garden.

Peterhouse   8 G1
Founded 1284 and the oldest College, Peterhouse is in Trumpington Street next to the Fitzwilliam Museum. The Poet Thomas Gray was entered here. There are windows by William Morris in Dining Hall. The College garden adjoins an old deer park, though now there are no animals.

Queens   8 F5
Founded in 1448 and situated in Queen's Lane it backs on to the Cam, Its foundress was Margaret of Anjou, Queen to Henry VI of England, hence the name of the College. Elizabeth Woodville, wife of Edward IV also endowed Queens' with the buildings surrounding the Second Court, which are most attractive.

Robinson   6 D4
Founded in 1977 by Mr David Robinson, and situated on Grange Road, this is the newest of the University Colleges.

St. Catharine's   8 G5
Founded 1473 is situated opposite Queens' across Queens Lane. Note the elegance of design and proportion.

St. John's   6 F3
Founded in 1511 and situated in New Court, the lawns sweep down to the river Cam. The Lady Margaret Beaufort, mother of Henry VII was the foundress of St. John's. The name derives from a Hospital of St. John formerly on that site.

Selwyn   8 D1
Founded 1882 is situated in Sidgwick Avenue.

Sidney Sussex   6 G3
Founded 1596 and situated between Sidney Street, Jesus Lane and King Street.

Trinity Hall   6 F4
Founded 1350 by the Bishop of Norwich but best known as a 'lawyer's college'.

Trinity   6 G4
Founded 1546 by Henry VIII at a time when he was enthusiastic for the 'new learning', it is next door to Trinity Hall in Trinity Lane. Its Great Court is the largest University Court in the world. The chapel tower is distinguished by a splendid gilt clock face. Byron was among famous writers entered here and his statue is in the Library.

Post Graduate Colleges

Hughes Hall (1885)	9	C1
St. Edmund's (1896)	15	E2
Darwin (1964)	8	F1
Wolfson (1965)	18	C1
Lucy Cavendish (1965)	15	E2
Clare Hall (1966)	15	D5

Other Places of Interest

Arts Theatre	6	G5
The Backs	6	F5
Botanic Garden	19	B4
Bridge of Sighs	6	F3
Cambridge United Football Club	17	A1
Cambridge City Football Ground	16	A1
Fenners-University Cricket Ground	9	C1
Fitzwilliam Museum	8	G1
Folk Museum	6	F3
Great St. Mary's Church	6	G4
Museum of Archaeology and Anthropology	9	A5
Museum of Classical Archaeology	8	E1
Museum of Geology	9	A5
Museum of Technology	16	E2
St. Bene't's Church	6	G5
Scott Polar Research Institute	9	B2
Sedgwick Museum	9	A5
Senate House	6	G4
Tourist Information Centre	6	G5
Whipple Museum	8	G5
Zoology Museum	8	G5

INDEX TO STREETS

General Abbreviations

Ave	Avenue	Gdns	Gardens	Pl	Place
Bri	Bridge	Grn	Green	Rd	Road
Clo	Close	Gro	Grove	Ri	Rise
Cres	Crescent	Ho	House	Sq	Square
Ct	Court	La	Lane	St	Street
Dr	Drive	Lo	Lodge	St.	Saint
Fld	Field	Ms	Mews	Ter	Terrace
Flds	Fields	Pas	Passage	Wk	Walk

A

Abbey Farm	10	E1
Abbey Rd.	16	D3
Abbey St.	16	E3
Abbey Wk.	16	E4
Abbots Clo.	13	A1
Acrefield Dr.	16	D2
Acton Way	12	F3
Adam & Eve St.	7	C5
Adams Rd.	15	C4
Addenbrooke's Hospital &		
Medical School	22	A5
Aingers Rd.	10	E3
Ainsworth Ct.	16	E5
Ainsworth Pl.	19	E1
Ainsworth St.	19	E1
Airport Terminal	17	D2
Akeman St.	12	F4
Albemarle Way	13	A1
Albert St.	16	A1
Albion Row	15	F2
Alex Wood Rd.	13	A2
Alice Way	10	G1
All Saints Pas.	6	G4
Alliance Ct.	22	B2
Allington Clo.	10	F1
Almoners Ave.	22	D5
Alpha Rd.	15	G1
Alpha Ter.	21	C4
Alstead Rd.	10	F1
Ancaster Way	20	A2
Angler's Way	13	G4
Ann's Rd.	14	E4
Antelope Way	20	G2
Applecourt	19	A5
Apthorpe Way	13	E1
Aragon Clo.	13	B1
Arbury	12	G2
Arbury Camp Farm	11	G4
Arbury Rd.	13	A1
Archway Ct.	18	D2
Argyle St.	19	E2
Arran Clo.	20	F4
Arthur St.	15	F1
Arts Theatre	6	G5
Arundel Clo.	12	E3
Ascham Rd.	13	B5
Ashbury Clo.	19	F5

Ashfield Rd.	13	F4
Ashvale	13	A1
Atherton Clo.	13	B5
Atkins Clo.	13	E1
Auckland Rd.	7	C3
Augers Rd.	20	F4
Aylesborough Clo.	12	G1
Aylestone Rd.	16	C2

B

Backs, The	6	F5
Badminton Clo.	12	F3
Bailey Ms.	7	C3
Bakery Clo.	14	D2
Baldock Way	22	B1
Bancroft Clo.	19	E5
Banhams Clo.	16	B2
Banoon Rd.	12	A2
Barnard Way	12	G3
Barnes Clo.	17	C2
Barnwell Business Park	17	C2
Barnwell Rd.	17	B4
Barrow Clo.	21	E2
Barrow Rd.	21	D1
Barrowcrofts	10	E1
Barton Clo.	18	C2
Bateman Ms.	19	B3
Bateman St.	19	A3
Bateson Rd.	12	G5
Baycliffe Clo.	20	B5
Beales Way	13	D1
Beaulands Clo.	16	C2
Beaumont Cres.	22	E4
Beaumont Rd.	22	E4
Beche Rd.	16	E3
Belgrave Rd.	19	G2
Bell Hill	10	E2
Belmont Pl.	7	B4
Belmore Clo.	12	F3
Belvoir Rd.	16	C2
Belvoir Ter.	19	A3
Bene't St	6	G5
Benson Pl.	15	E1
Benson St.	15	E1
Bentinck St.	9	B2
Bentley Rd.	21	E1
Bergholt Clo.	14	D4
Bermuda Rd.	12	F5

Bermuda Ter.	12	F5
Beverly Way	21	B5
Bin Brook	15	C5
Birch Clo.	13	D3
Bird Sanctuary	20	C4
Birdwood Rd.	20	A2
Bishop Way	10	G4
Blackhall Rd.	12	F1
Blanford Wk.	12	F1
Blenheim Clo.	20	C5
Blinco Gro.	22	A1
Bliss Way	20	F3
Blossom St.	7	D5
Blue Boar Hotel	6	G4
Borrowdale	12	F3
Botolph La.	8	G5
Bourne Rd.	14	A2
Bowers Cft.	22	D5
Bower's Farm	10	C5
Brackenbury	10	G5
Brackley Clo.	13	A2
Brackyn Rd.	19	F3
Bradbrushe Fields	15	A1
Bradmore La.	7	C5
Bradmore St.	7	C5
Brambles, The, Girton	12	B2
Brampton Rd.	16	F5
Brandon Pl.	7	C4
Brentwood Clo.	14	E4
Bridewell Rd.	20	F4
Bridge of Sighs	6	F3
Bridge Rd.	11	G1
Bridge St.	6	G3
Brierley Wk.	12	F1
Brimley Rd.	13	A3
Britten Pl.	20	A2
Broad St.	7	C5
Brookfields	20	A1
Brookfields Hospital	19	G2
Brooklands Ave.	19	B4
Brooks Rd.	17	A5
Brookside	9	A2
Brookside La.	19	A2
Brownlow Rd.	12	F1
Broxbourne Clo.	20	G3
Brunswick Gdns.	7	B3
Brunswick Ter.	7	C3
Brunswick Wk.	7	B3
Buckingham Rd.	15	E1
Budleigh Clo.	20	A1
Buffalo Way	20	G2
Bulstrode Gdns.	15	C2
Burkett Way	10	F1
Burleigh Pl.	7	C4
Burleigh St.	7	C4
Burnham Clo.	20	F3
Burnside	20	A1
Burrell's Wk.	6	D4
Burrough Field	11	G2
Bus Station	7	A4
Butler Way	13	A2
Butt Grn.	7	B3
Byron Sq.	21	C5

C

Cadwin Fld.	13	C1
Cam Causeway	13	G3
Cam (or Granta), River	14	A3
Cambridge Airport	17	E3
Cambridge Business Park	13	G1
Cambridge City Football Club	16	A1
Cambridge Darkroom	9	D1
Cambridge Pl.	9	B2
Cambridge Rd., Girton	11	B3
Cambridge Rd., Impington	11	G2
Cambridge Rd., Impington	11	G4
Cambridge Rugby Football Ground	18	B3
Cambridge United Football Club	17	A1
Cambridge University Press	21	F1
Cambridgeshire High School For Girls	21	G4
Camden Ct.	9	B5
Cameron Rd.	13	C1
Campbell La.	21	B5
Campbell St.	19	E2
Campkin Rd.	13	C1
Camside	13	E5
Cannon Cinema	9	A5
Canterbury Clo.	12	E5
Canterbury St.	12	E5
Capstan Clo.	16	D2
Caribou Way	20	G1
Carisbrooke Rd.	12	E3
Carlton Way	12	G4
Carlyle Rd.	15	G1
Caroline Pl.	7	C4
Castle Ct.	15	F1
Castle Mound	15	F2
Castle Row	15	F2
Castle St.	15	F1
Catherine St.	19	F2
Causeway Pas.	7	C3
Cavendish Ave.	22	B2
Cavendish Laboratory	15	B3
Cavendish Rd.	19	E2
Cawcutt's Farm	11	G3
Cenacle, The	18	E3
Chalfont Clo.	20	D3
Chalk Gro.	22	E4
Chalmers Rd.	20	A3
Champneys Wk.	18	D2
Chantry Clo.	16	C1
Chapel St.	13	E5
Chartfield Rd.	20	E3
Chatsworth Ave.	12	E3
Chaucer Clo.	19	A4
Chaucer Rd.	18	G4
Cheddars La.	16	F2
Chedworth St.	18	E3
Chelwood Rd.	20	D3
Chemical Laboratories	9	A2
Chequers Rd.	10	G5
Cherry Bounds Rd.	11	A4
Cherry Clo.	20	D5

Cherry Hinton	20	E3
Cherry Hinton Rd.	19	E5
Cherry Hinton Rd.	20	G2
Chesterfield Rd.	13	E3
Chesterton	13	D4
Chesterton Hall Cres.	13	C5
Chesterton Hospital	13	D5
Chesterton La.	15	F2
Chesterton Rd.	16	A1
Chestnut Gro.	13	C5
Chetney Way	14	A2
Chigwell Ct.	14	D4
Chivers Way	10	F5
Christ Church St.	7	C3
Christ's College	7	A4
Christ's La.	7	A4
Christ's Pieces	7	A4
Church End	20	E1
Church End (Road)	20	E1
Church La., Girton	11	A4
Church La., Trumpington	21	B5
Church Rate Wk.	8	E2
Church Rd., Teversham	17	G3
Church St., Chesterton	16	E1
Church St., Histon	10	E2
Church St., Fen Ditton	14	D2
Churchill College	15	C1
City Rd.	7	C4
Clare Bri.	6	F4
Clare College	6	F4
Clare College Playing Fields	21	F1
Clare Hall	15	D5
Clare College Memorial Court	6	E4
Clare Rd.	8	E2
Clare St.	15	F1
Claremont	19	C3
Clarendon Rd.	19	C4
Clarendon St.	7	B5
Clarkson Clo.	15	D3
Clarkson Rd.	15	C3
Clay Close La.		
Clay St.	10	F1
Claygate Rd.	20	E3
Clifton Rd.	19	D5
Cliveden Clo.	12	E3
Clover Ct.	20	G5
Cockburn St.	19	E2
Cockcroft Pl.	15	D3
Cockerell Rd.	12	G3
Cockerton Rd.	11	B2
Coe Fen	8	E2
Coggeshall Clo.	14	D4
Coldham's Common	17	A2
Coldham's Gro.	17	A4
Coldham's La.	16	F4
Coldham's Rd.	16	F4
Coleridge Recreation Ground	19	E4
Coleridge Rd.	19	F3
College of Art & Technology	9	D5
College Rd.	11	F2
Collier Rd.	9	C5
Coltsfoot Clo.	20	G5
Colville Rd.	20	E4
Colwyn Clo.	12	G4
Comfrey Ct.	20	G5
Community College	7	B5
Conduit Head Rd.	15	A1
Coniston Rd.	22	C1
Coppice, The	11	G2
Corfe Clo.	21	G1
Corn Exchange St.	6	G5
Corona Rd.	16	A1
Coronation St.	19	B2
Corpus Christi College	8	G5
Corpus Christi Sports Ground	15	C5
Corrie Rd.	19	E3
County Hall	7	A4
Courtland Ave.	22	D2
Courtney Way	13	A4
Covent Gdns.	9	C1
Cowper Rd.	19	F5
Cranleigh Clo.		
Cranmer Rd.	15	C5
Crathern Way	13	C1
Crescent Rd.	11	F2
Crispin Pl.	7	C4
Croft Clo.	10	E1
Croft Lo.	18	D2
Croft Holme La.	16	A1
Cromwell Ct.	7	A4
Cromwell Rd.	16	F5
Cross St.	9	C1
Crowland Way	13	C1
Crowthorne Clo.	20	D3
Cunningham Clo.	13	A3
Cutter Ferry Clo.	16	D2
Cyprus Rd.	19	G3

D

Dalton Sq.	13	F4
Dane Dr.	15	B5
Danesbury Ct.	19	G1
Darwin College	8	F1
Darwin Dr.	12	F4
Davey Clo.	10	G5
David St.	19	E2
Davy Rd.	19	E4
Daws Clo.	20	D3
Daws La.	20	C3
De Freville Ave.	16	C2
Dean Dr.	22	B3
Denis Wilson Ct.	21	D2
Dennis Rd.	14	E4
Derby Rd.	19	E5
Derby St.	18	E3
Derwent Clo.	20	A4
Desmond Ave.	20	D4
Devonshire Ct.	19	D2
Devonshire Rd.	19	D2
Diamond Rd.	21	E1
Ditton Flds.	14	B4
Ditton La.	14	D4
Ditton Wk.	14	A4
Dodford La.	11	A2
Doggett Rd.	20	D3
Dolphin Clo.	20	G2

Dover St.	7	C5
Dowding Way	12	G3
Downham's La.	13	D3
Downing College	9	A1
Downing Pl.	9	A5
Downing St.	9	G5
Drayton Clo.	20	F5
Drayton Rd.	20	F5
Drosier Rd.	9	B1
Drummer St.	7	A4
Duck End	11	A4
Dudley Rd.	14	C4
Dundee Clo.	13	F4
Dunsmore Clo.	14	D3
Durnford Way	13	B3
Dwyer-Joyce Clo.	10	F3

E

Eachard Rd.	12	D4
Earl St.	7	B4
East Hertford St.	15	G2
East Rd.	7	C5
Eastfield	13	F4
Eden St.	7	B4
Eden St. Backway	7	B4
Edendale Clo.	22	C2
Edinburgh Rd.	13	E4
Edward St.	16	D5
Edwinstowe Clo.	18	G4
Egerton Clo.	14	C4
Egerton Rd.	14	C4
Ekin Rd.	14	C5
Elfleda Rd.	14	A5
Elizabeth Way	16	D1
Ellesmere Rd.	13	A1
Elm St.	7	B4
Elmfield	13	E4
Elmfield Clo.	13	E4
Elsworth Pl.	19	D5
Eltisley Ave.	18	E3
Emery Rd.	9	D1
Emery St.	9	D1
Emmanuel College	7	A5
Emmanuel College Sports Ground	15	B3
Emmanuel Rd.	7	B4
Emmanuel St.	7	A5
Engineering Laboratories	8	G2
Ennisdale Rd.	13	B1
Enniskillen Rd.	13	F4
Essex Clo.	13	A3
Evelyn Hospital, The	19	A5

F

Fair Ct.	7	B4
Fair St.	7	B4
Fairbairn Rd.	14	A2
Fairfax Rd.	19	F1
Fairway	11	A1
Fallowfield	13	G4

Fanshawe Rd.	19	E4
Farmstead Clo.	10	F1
Farringford Clo.	12	F3
Felton St.	9	D1
Fen Causeway, The	8	F2
Fen Ditton	14	E2
Fen Rd.	14	B2
Fendon Clo.	22	C4
Fendon Rd.	22	C4
Fennec Clo.	20	G3
Fenners University Cricket Ground	9	C1
Ferndale Ri.	14	A4
Fernlea Clo.	20	E3
Ferrars Way	12	G2
Ferry La.	13	F5
Ferry Path	16	B2
Field Way	22	D5
Finch Rd.	12	G3
Fire Station	9	C5
First Ct.	7	A4
Fisher St.	15	G1
Fisher's La.	20	E4
Fison Rd.	14	E3
Fitzroy La.	7	C4
Fitzroy St.	7	B4
Fitzwilliam College	15	D1
Fitzwilliam Hall Ground	12	D4
Fitzwilliam Museum	8	G1
Fitzwilliam Rd.	19	C5
Fitzwilliam St.	8	G1
Flamsteed Rd.	19	E5
Fletcher's Ter	19	E2
Flower St.	7	D5
Folk Museum	15	F3
Fontwell Ave.	12	E3
Footpath, The (Histon)	10	F1
Fordwich Clo.	12	G2
Forest Rd.	20	D5
Fortescue Rd.	13	A2
Francis Darwin Ct.	12	F4
Frank's La.	13	G4
Fraser Rd.	13	E3
Free School La.	8	G5
French's Rd.	12	F5
Friar's Clo.	20	D5
Fulbourn Hospital	20	G5
Fulbourn Old Drift	20	F3
Fulbourn Rd.	20	E5
Fulbrooke Rd.	18	B2

G

Gainsborough Clo.	13	G2
Galfrid Rd.	17	B1
Garden House Hotel	8	G1
Garden Wk., Histon	10	G1
Garden Wk., New Chesterton	12	G5
Garlic Row	16	G2
Garret Hostel La.	6	F4
Gayton Clo.	21	C5
Gazeley Rd.	21	C3
Gazelle Way	20	G1

Geldart St.	16	D4
GPO Sorting Office	9	C5
Geodesy & Geophysics	15	A1
George Pateman Ct.	19	C3
George St.	13	B5
George IV St.	9	B2
Gerard Clo.	17	B1
Gifford Pl.	6	G4
Gifford's Clo.	11	A4
Gilbert Clo.	12	F3
Gilbert Rd.	12	G4
Girton	11	C3
Gisborne Rd.	19	G4
Gladstone Way	20	D5
Glebe Rd.	22	B2
Glenacre Clo.	20	D5
Glenmere Clo.	20	B5
Glisson Rd.	9	C2
Godesdone Rd.	16	E3
Godwin Clo.	22	E3
Godwin Way	22	D3
Golding Rd.	19	F4
Golf Course, Girton	11	A1
Gonville and Caius College	6	G4
Gonville Hotel	9	B1
Gonville Pl.	9	B1
Gough Way	15	B5
Gowers, The	11	A3
Grafton Cen.	7	C4
Grafton St.	7	C4
Grange Rd.	6	D5
Granta Pl.	8	F1
Grantchester Meadows	18	D4
Grantchester Rd.	18	B5
Grantchester Rd., Trumpington	21	A5
Grantchester St.	18	E3
Grasmere Gdns.	15	G1
Gray Rd.	20	A3
Grayling Clo.	13	E5
Great Eastern St.	19	E2
Great St. Mary's Church	6	G4
Green, The, Chesterton	13	G3
Green, The, Histon	10	F3
Green End, Fen Ditton	14	D1
Green End Rd.	13	F2
Green Pk.	13	G2
Green St.	6	G4
Greenhouse Farm	14	G5
Greenleas	10	F1
Green's Rd.	16	A1
Gresham Rd.	9	B1
Gretton Ct.	11	A3
Greville Rd.	19	E3
Greystoke Ct.	20	C5
Greystoke Rd.	20	C5
Grove, The	13	G3
Guest Rd.	9	C1
Guildhall	6	G5
Guildhall St.	6	G4
Gunhild Clo.	20	A5
Gunhild Ct.	20	A5
Gunhild Way	20	A5
Gunning Way	12	F3
Gurney Rd.	13	B5
Gwydir St.	19	D1

H

Hale Ave.	12	G5
Hale St.	15	F1
Halifax Rd.	12	D5
Hall Farm	14	D2
Hall Farm Rd.	12	G3
Hamilton Rd.	16	C1
Harcombe Rd.	20	D3
Harding Way, Arbury	12	F3
Harding Way, Histon	10	E2
Harebell Clo.	20	F5
Hardwick St.	18	E3
Harris Rd.	12	G3
Hartington Gro.	22	A1
Harvest Way	16	E3
Harvey Ct.	8	E5
Harvey Goodwin Ave.	12	G5
Harvey Rd.	9	B2
Hatherdene Clo.	20	D1
Havenfield	13	C3
Haviland Way	13	D2
Hawkins Rd.	13	D2
Hawthorn Way	16	C1
Haymarket Rd.	15	F2
Hayster Dr.	20	D3
Hazelwood Clo.	12	F1
HPO	7	A5
Headford Clo.	14	C4
Headington Clo.	20	E5
Headington Dr.	20	E5
Health Centre	14	D4
Hedgerley Clo.	15	B2
Helen Clo.	14	D4
Hemingford Rd.	19	F2
Henley Rd.	16	E3
Henry Morris Rd.	10	G5
Herbert St.	13	B5
Hereward Clo.	10	G4
Heron's Clo.	22	E4
Herschel Rd.	15	D4
Hertford St.	15	F1
Hick's La.	11	A4
High Ditch St.	14	F3
High St., Chesterton	13	F5
High St., Cherry Hinton	20	E3
High St., Fen Ditton	14	D2
High St., Girton	11	A3
High St., Histon	10	F3
High St., Trumpington	21	B5
Highdene Rd.	20	F3
Highfield Ave.	13	B3
Highfield Rd.	11	F3
Highworth Ave.	13	C4
Hilda St.	15	G1
Hills Ave.	22	B2
Hills Rd.	19	B2
Hinton Ave.	22	C2
Histon	10	F3
Histon Rd.	12	F4
Hoadly Rd.	12	D3

Hobart Rd.	19	G3
Hobson St.	7	A4
Hobson's Pas.	6	G4
Holbrook Rd.	22	B3
Holland St.	15	G1
Holy Sepulchre Church	6	G3
Holyrood Clo.	12	E2
Home Clo.	10	E4
Home Farm	14	F3
Homerton College	21	G1
Homerton St.	19	C5
Homing, The	17	D1
Honey Hill	15	F2
Hooper St.	19	E1
Hope St.	19	F2
Hopkins Clo.	13	E2
Howard Clo.	14	B3
Howard Rd.	14	C3
Howes Clo.	12	B2
Howes Pl.	12	C3
Hughes Hall	9	C1
Hulatt Rd.	22	D3
Humberston Rd.	16	C2
Humphreys Rd.	13	A2
Huntingdon Rd.	12	A2
Huntley Clo.	14	D3
Hurrell Rd.	12	F3
Hurst Park Ave.	13	B4

I

Impala Dr.	20	G2
Impington	11	E1
Impington La.	10	G3
Inverness Clo.	13	E4
Iver Clo.	20	E2
Izaak Walton Way	13	G4

J

Jackson Rd.	13	D1
James St.	7	C3
Jermyn Clo.	12	G2
Jesus College	7	A3
Jesus Grn.	16	A2
Jesus La.	7	A3
John Clarke Ct.	13	D3
John St.	7	C4
Jolley Way	13	D2

K

Kay Hitch Way	10	F5
Keates Rd.	20	F5
Kelsey Cres.	20	G2
Kelvin Clo.	20	A4
Kendal Way	13	F3
Kent Way	13	D2
Kerridge Clo.	19	E1
Keynes Rd.	14	C4
Kimberley Rd.	16	C2

King St.	7	A4
King's & Selwyn College Sports Ground	18	A2
King's Bridge	6	F5
King's College	6	G5
King's College Chapel	6	G4
King's College Choir School	6	E5
King's College Fellows Garden	6	E5
King's College Hostel	6	E5
King's Hedges Rd.	11	G5
King's La.	8	G5
King's Par.	8	G5
King's Rd.	18	D3
King's School Playing Fld.	6	D5
Kingston St.	19	D1
Kingsway	10	F2
Kinnaird Way	22	D4
Kinross Rd.	13	D4
Kirkby Clo.	13	D4

L

Laburnum Clo.	13	D5
Lady Jane Ct.	22	A1
Lady Margaret Rd.	15	E2
Lambourn Clo.	21	B5
Lammas Field	18	E3
Lammas Land	8	F2
Langdale Clo.	20	F2
Langham Rd.	19	G4
Larkin Clo.	13	D2
Latham Clo.	18	G4
Latham Rd.	18	G4
Latimer Clo.	17	C1
Laundress La.	8	F5
Lavender Rd.	13	D1
Lawrence Way	13	D1
Lees Way	11	A3
Leete Rd.	20	F5
Lensfield Rd.	9	A2
Lent's Way	14	A2
Leonard Clo.	14	E4
Lexington Clo.	12	E3
Leyburn Clo.	20	F2
Leys Ave.	13	C3
Leys Rd.	13	C4
Leys School	8	G2
Lichfield Rd.	19	F5
Lilac Ct.	22	D1
Limekiln Rd.	22	G4
Linden Clo.	12	F5
Lingholme Clo.	12	E4
Lingrey Ct.	21	C5
Lion Yard Shopping Centre	6	G4
Lisle Wk.	20	F3
Little St. Mary's La.	8	G1
Local Examination Syndicate	9	B1
Logan's Way	16	E2
Lomas Farm	14	C1
Long Reach Ho.	14	C2
Long Reach Rd.	14	A2
Long Rd.	21	D3
Lone Tree Ave.	11	F3

Loris Ct.	20	G2
Love La.	20	D4
Lovell Rd.	13	F1
Love's Clo	10	F5
Lower Park St.	6	G3
Luard Clo.	21	G2
Luard Rd.	21	G2
Lucerne Clo.	20	F4
Lucketts Clo.	10	F2
Lucy Cavendish College	15	E2
Lyndewode Rd.	9	C2
Lynfield La.	16	E1
Lynx, The	20	G2

M

Macfarlane Rd.	10	G5
Mackenzie Rd.	9	D1
Madingley Rd.	15	A1
Madras Rd.	19	G3
Magdalene College	6	F3
Magdalene College Sports Ground	13	C3
Magdalene St.	6	F3
Magnolia Clo.	22	C1
Magrath Ave.	15	F1
Maids Causeway	7	B3
Maitland Ave.	13	G2
Malcolm St.	7	A3
Mallards, The	16	E2
Mallets Rd.	20	F5
Malta Rd.	19	F3
Malting La.	8	F1
Maltsters Way	13	E5
Malvern Rd.	20	D4
Mandrill Clo.	20	G2
Maners Way	22	D4
Manhattan Dr.	16	C2
Manor Farm, Girton	10	B5
Manor Pk.	10	D2
Manor St.	7	A4
Mansel Way	13	B2
Maple Clo.	13	D5
March La.	20	F1
Marfield Ct.	13	C4
Mariners Way	16	D2
Marion Clo.	12	D5
Maris La.	21	B5
Market Hill	6	G4
Market Pas.	6	G4
Market St.	6	G4
Mark's Way	11	B3
Marlowe Rd.	18	D3
Marshall Rd.	22	A1
Mawson Rd.	9	C2
Mayfield Rd.	11	C5
Mays Way	14	A2
Meadow Farm	10	C1
Meadowlands Rd.	17	D1
Melbourne Pl.	7	B5
Melvin Way	10	C2
Mercer's Row	16	G1
Mere Way	13	A2
Merton Hall	6	F3
Merton Rd.	10	E3
Merton St.	18	E3
Metcalfe Rd.	13	A4
Michaels Clo.	11	A3
Midhurst Clo.	13	F5
Midsummer Common	7	B3
Midwinter Pl.	16	C1
Mill End Clo.	20	D4
Mill End Rd.	20	D4
Mill La.	8	G1
Mill La., Histon	10	G2
Mill Pit	8	F1
Mill Rd., Barnwell	9	C1
Mill Rd., Impington	11	F2
Mill St.	9	C1
Millington Rd.	18	D3
Milton Rd.	13	B5
Milton's Wk.	7	A4
Missleton Ct.	20	A5
Molewood Clo.	12	F2
Monkswell	21	G5
Montague Rd.	16	C1
Montfort Way	13	B2
Montgomery Rd.	13	B3
Montreal Rd.	20	A1
Montreal Sq.	19	G3
Montrose Clo.	13	B1
Mortimer Rd.	9	C1
Mortlock Ave.	13	G2
Moss Bank	14	A2
Mount Pleasant	15	E2
Mount Pleasant Wk.	15	E2
Mowbray Rd.	22	C3
Mowlam Clo.	10	G5
Moyne Clo.	13	A1
Mulberry Clo.	13	C4
Museum of Archaeology & Anthropology	9	A5
Museum of Classical Archaeology	8	E1
Museum of Geology	9	A5
Museum of Technology	16	F2
Musgrave Way	14	F1

N

Napier St.	7	C3
Narrow Clo.	10	G1
Narrow La.	10	F2
Natal Rd.	20	A1
National Institute ofl Agricultural Botany	12	B3
Neale Clo.	20	F2
Nelson Clo.	7	D4
Nelson St.	7	D4
Netherhall Farm	22	E5
Netherhall Way	22	E4
Neville Rd.	19	G5
New Chesterton	13	A5
New Ct.	6	F3
New Hall	15	E1
New Park St.	6	G3

New Rd., Histon	10	A2
New Rd., Impington	11	G1
New School Rd.	10	F4
New Sq.	7	B4
New St.	7	D4
Newell Wk.	20	E2
Newmarket Rd.	16	F3
Newnham	15	A4
Newnham College	8	D1
Newnham Croft St.	18	E2
Newnham Rd.	8	F2
Newnham Wk.	8	E1
Newton Rd.	21	E1
Newtown	19	A3
Nicholson Way	13	B2
Nightingale Ave.	22	C5
Norfolk St.	7	C4
Norfolk Ter.	7	D5
Normanton Way	10	F1
North Cotts.	21	C3
North Ct.	7	A4
North St.	15	E1
North Ter.	7	B3
Northampton St.	6	F3
Northern By-pass	11	E4
Northfield Ave.	13	B1
Northfield Rd.	11	A1
Northumberland Clo.	13	A2
Norton Clo.	17	B1
Norwich St.	19	B3
Nuffield Rd.	13	G3
Nun's Orchard	10	F1
Nursery Wk.	12	E4
Nutting's Rd.	17	B4

O

Oak Tree Ave.	13	D4
Oates Way	10	F1
Occupation Rd.	16	D3
Old Farm Clo.	10	F1
Old Schools	6	G4
Orchard Ave.	13	B4
Orchard Clo.	11	B3
Orchard Est.	20	E2
Orchard Rd.	10	G2
Orchard St.	7	B4
Owlstone Rd.	18	E3
Oxford Rd.	12	D5
Oyster Row.	16	F2

P

Paddocks, The	17	A4
Paget Clo.	21	D5
Paget Rd.	21	C5
Pakenham Clo.	13	D4
Palmers Wk.	9	C5
Pamplin Ct.	20	E3
Panther Way	20	G2
Panton St.	9	A2
Paradise St.	7	C4

Park Ave.	10	E3
Park Farm	10	D4
Park La.	10	D2
Park Par.	6	G3
Park St.	6	G3
Park Ter.	9	A5
Parker Ter.	7	D4
Parker St.	7	B5
Parker's Piece	9	B5
Parkside	9	B5
Parr Clo.	10	G4
Parson's Ct.	6	G5
Parsonage St.	7	C3
Peacock Way	10	G1
Pearce Clo.	18	C1
Peas Hill	6	G5
Pemberton Ter.	19	A2
Pembroke College	8	G5
Pembroke Sports Ground	18	C3
Pembroke St.	8	G5
Pen Clo.	20	F4
Penarth Pl.	18	B1
Pentlands Clo.	16	C2
Pepys Ter.	11	G2
Pepys Way	11	B5
Perne Ave.	19	G5
Perne Rd.	19	G5
Perowne St.	9	D1
Perse Preparatory School	21	D2
Perse School	22	A3
Perse Way	12	G3
Peter's Fld.	9	C5
Peterhouse	8	G1
Petty Cury	6	G4
Petworth St.	16	D4
Peverel Clo.	17	C1
Peverel Rd.	17	C1
Pike's Wk.	7	A4
Pine Ct.	11	G1
Pinehurst	18	D1
Police Station	9	C5
Poplar Rd.	10	F5
Porson Ct.	21	D2
Porson Rd.	21	D2
Portland Pl.	7	B4
Portugal Pl.	6	G3
Post Office Ter.	7	A5
Pound Hill	15	F2
Pretoria Rd.	16	B2
Primary Ct.	13	F5
Primrose St.	16	A1
Prior's Clo.	10	F2
Priory Rd.	16	D3
Priory St.	15	E1
Prospect Row	7	B4
Purbeck Rd.	21	G1

Q

Quainton Clo.	14	B5
Quayside	6	G3
Queen Edith's Way	22	B4
Queens' Bridge	8	F5

Queens' College 8 F5
Queens' Grn. 8 F5
Queens' La. 8 F5
Queen's Meadow 20 E2
Queen's Rd. 8 E4
Queen's Sports Ground 18 A2
Queensway 19 A5

R

Rachel Clo. 14 E4
Rackham Clo. 12 F5
Radegund Rd. 19 F4
Railway Station 19 D3
Railway St. 20 E3
Ramsden Sq. 13 E2
Rathmore Clo. 19 D5
Rathmore Rd. 22 A1
Rawlyn Clo. 17 B1
Rawlyn Rd. 17 B1
Rayleigh Clo. 21 E1
Rayson Way 17 B1
Red Cross La. 22 B5
Red Gate Rd. 11 B4
Redfern Clo. 13 B3
Regatta Ct. 16 F1
Regent St. 9 A1
Regent Ter. 9 B1
Richmond Rd. 12 D5
Rickard Clo. 20 D3
Ridley Hall 8 E1
Ridley Hall Rd. 8 F1
River La. 16 E3
Riverside 16 E2
Robert May Clo. 20 A2
Robert Jennings Clo. 13 E3
Robinson College 6 D4
Robinson Way 21 G5
Rock Rd. 22 B1
Rodings, The 14 E4
Roedeer Clo. 20 G2
Roland Clo. 13 A3
Romsey Rd. 19 G2
Romsey Ter. 19 F3
Romsey Town 19 G1
Ronald Rolph Ct. 14 B3
Rose Cres. 6 G4
Roseford Rd. 12 F2
Rosemary La. 20 D1
Ross St. 19 F2
Rotherwick Way 22 C5
Rothleigh Rd. 20 B5
Round Church St. 6 G3
Roxburgh Rd. 13 B1
Royal Cambridge Hotel 9 A2
Rush Gro. 20 G3
Russell Ct. 19 A3
Russell St. 19 B3
Rustat Rd. 19 E4
Rutherford Rd. 21 E3
Rutland Clo. 12 G2

S

Sable Clo. 20 G2
Sackville Clo. 13 B1
Saffron Rd. 10 F4
St. Albans Rd. 12 G2
St. Andrew's Glebe 20 F2
St. Andrew's Pk. 10 E1
St. Andrew's Rd. 16 D2
St. Andrew's St. 9 A5
St. Audrey's Clo. 10 D3
St. Barnabas Rd. 9 D2
St. Bede's Cres. 20 C3
St. Bede's Gdns. 20 C3
St. Benet's Church 6 G5
St. Catharine's College 8 G5
St. Christopher's Ave. 12 E5
St. Edmund's College 15 E2
St. Eligius St. 19 A3
St. Faith's School 19 A5
St. John's Bri. 6 F3
St. John's College 6 F3
St. John's College Sports Ground 6 E3
St. John's Rd. 6 G3
St. John's St. 6 G4
St. Kilda Ave. 13 D1
St. Luke's St. 15 F1
St. Margaret's Rd. 12 A1
St. Margaret's Sq. 22 C1
St. Mark's Ct. 18 D2
St. Mary's St. 6 G4
St. Matthew's St. 7 D4
St. Paul's Rd. 9 B2
St. Paul's Wk. 9 B2
St. Peter's St. 15 F2
St. Peter's Ter. 8 G1
St. Philip's Rd. 19 F2
St. Stephen's Pl. 12 E5
St. Thomas's Rd. 20 B3
St. Thomas's Sq. 20 B3
St. Tibb's Row 6 A5
St. Vincent's Clo. 11 A5
Salmon La. 7 B4
Sandy La. 16 C1
Saxon Rd. 16 E3
Saxon St. 9 A2
School La. 10 G5
School Hill 10 F2
School of Veterinary Medicine 15 A2
Scotland Clo. 13 F5
Scotland Rd. 13 E5
Scotsdowne Rd. 21 C5
Scott Polar Research Institute 9 B2
Searle St. 15 G1
Sedgwick Museum 9 A5
Sedgwick St. 19 E2
Sedley Taylor Rd. 21 G2
Sefton Clo. 21 C4
Selwyn College 8 D1
Selwyn Gdns. 18 D1
Selwyn Rd. 18 C2
Senate Ho. 6 G4

Senate House Pas.	6	G4
Severn Pl.	7	D4
Seymour St.	19	G2
Shaftesbury Rd.	19	B4
Sheep's Grn.	8	F2
Shelley Row	15	F2
Shelly Garden	15	F2
Shepherd's Clo.	20	F4
Sherbourne Ct.	13	F3
Sherbourne Clo.	13	G3
Sherlock Clo.	12	D4
Sherlock Rd.	12	D4
Shire Hall	15	F2
Shirley Gro.	13	F3
Shirley Rd.	10	E3
Short St.	7	B4
Sidgwick Ave.	8	D1
Sidney Farm Rd.	20	D3
Sidney St.	6	G4
Sidney Sussex College	6	G3
Silver St.	8	F1
Silverwood Clo.	16	E4
Sleaford St.	16	E5
Smart's Row	7	D4
Somerset Clo.	13	A1
Somerset Rd.	10	E3
South Cambridgeshire District Council Offices	9	B2
South Green Rd.	18	D3
South Rd.	11	F2
Southacre Dr.	18	G4
Southacre Clo.	19	A4
Southbrooke Clo.	21	C5
Spalding Way	22	E3
Speedwell Clo.	20	G4
Spens Ave.	18	C1
Spring Clo.	10	G2
Springfield Rd.	16	B1
Springfield Ter.	16	B1
Staffordshire St.	7	D4
Stanesfield Clo.	17	B1
Stanesfield Rd.	17	B1
Stanley Rd.	16	F1
Stansgate Ave.	22	B5
Station Rd., Histon	10	F3
Station Rd., Newtown	19	C3
Sterndale Clo.	11	B4
Sterne Clo.	19	E5
Stirling Clo.	13	E4
Stockwell St.	19	E2
Stone St.	16	E5
Storey's Way	12	C5
Stourbridge Common	13	G5
Stourbridge Gro.	16	G5
Strangeways Rd.	22	E3
Stratfield Clo.	12	E3
Stretton Ave.	12	G5
Student Health Centre	9	C1
Stukeley Clo.	18	B1
Sturton St.	19	E1
Suez Rd.	19	G3
Summerfield	8	E2
Sun St.	7	D3
Sunmead Wk.	20	F3
Sunnyside	17	D2
Sussex St.	6	G4
Swann's Rd.	16	G1
Swann's Ter.	19	E2
Swimming Pool	16	A2
Swimming Pool	9	C1
Sylvester Rd.	15	C4
Symonds Clo.	10	F2

T

Tavistock Rd.	12	E3
Tamarin Gdns.	20	G3
Taunton Clo.	20	A2
Teasel Way	20	G4
Tedder Way	12	F2
Tenby Clo.	20	F3
Tenison Ave.	19	C2
Tenison Ct.	9	D2
Tenison Rd.	9	D2
Tennis Court Rd.	9	A5
Tennis Court Ter.	8	G1
TA Centre	20	A5
TA Centre	17	B5
Teversham	17	G3
Teversham Drift	20	F1
Teynham Clo.	20	A1
Thetford Ter.	17	D1
Thirleby Clo.	12	G3
Thoday St.	19	F2
Thompson's La.	6	G3
Thorleye Rd.	17	B1
Thornton Clo.	12	B2
Thornton Ct.	12	A2
Thornton Rd.	12	A1
Thornton Way	12	B1
Thorpe Way	14	D5
Thrift's Wk.	13	F5
Tillyard Way	22	F3
Tiptree Clo.	14	E4
Tiverton Way	20	A2
Topcliffe Way	22	D4
Topham Way	12	G3
Trafalgar St.	16	B1
Tredegar Clo.	13	B2
Trevone Pl.	20	A2
Trinity Bri.	6	F4
Trinity College	6	G4
Trinity College Fellows Garden	6	E4
Trinity College Ground	15	D3
Trinity Hall College	6	F4
Trinity Hall Sports Ground	12	D5
Trinity La.	6	G4
Trinity New Fld.	18	C3
Trinity St.	6	G4
Trumpington	21	D4
Trumpington Hall	21	A4
Trumpington Rd.	21	D2
Trumpington St.	8	G1

U

Union La.	13	D4
Union Rd.	9	A2
University Arms Hotel	9	B5
University Botanic Garden	19	B4
University Centre	8	G1
University Farm	12	B5
University LTC	9	C2
University Library	6	E4
University Music School	8	E5
University Observatory	15	B1
University Rugby Ground	15	D5
Uphall Rd.	17	B4
Upper Gwydir St.	16	D5

V

Valerian Ct.	20	G4
Velos Wk.	14	D4
Ventress Clo.	20	B5
Verulam Way	13	A1
Vicarage Ter.	16	D4
Victoria Ave.	7	B3
Victoria Pk.	15	G1
Victoria Rd.	15	F1
Victoria St.	7	B4
Villa Pl.	11	F1
Villa Rd.	11	F1
Vinery Rd.	19	G2
Vinery Way	19	G1
Violet Clo.	20	F5
Vision Pk.	11	F1

W

Wadloes Footpath	14	D3
Wadloes Rd.	14	C4
Walnut Tree Ave.	7	D3
Walpole Rd.	20	B4
Ward Rd.	20	A3
Warkworth St.	9	B5
Warkworth Ter.	9	B5
Warren Rd.	13	E3
Warwick Rd.	12	E4
Washpit Rd.	11	A3
Water La., Chesterton	13	F5
Water La., Histon	10	F3
Water St.	13	F5
Wavell Way	13	A3
Wellington Pas.	7	D3
Wellington St.	7	D3
Welstead Rd.	20	F3
Wentworth Rd.	12	E4
Wenvoe Clo.	20	E4
Wesley Ho.	7	A3
West Gdns.	8	D5
West Rd.	8	E5
West Rd., Histon	10	F3
Westcott Ho.	7	A3
Westering, The	17	D1

Westfield La.	12	E5
Westfield Rd.	12	E5
Westminster College	6	E3
Wetenhall Rd.	19	E1
Wheeler St.	6	G5
Whipple Museum	8	G5
Whitehill Clo.	17	B2
Whitehill Rd.	17	A1
Whitehouse La.	12	B3
Whitfield Clo.	13	C1
Whittle Laboratory	15	B2
Whyman's La.	15	F2
Wilberforce Rd.	15	C3
Wilderspin Clo.	12	A1
Wilding Wk.	13	E5
Wiles Clo.	13	D1
Wilkin St.	9	C2
William Smith Ct.	19	E3
Willis Rd.	9	C5
Willow Pl.	7	B4
Willow Wk.	7	B4
Wilson Clo.	13	D2
Winchmore Dr.	21	B4
Windermere Clo.	20	F2
Winders La.	10	F1
Windlesham Clo.	13	B2
Windmill La.	10	F2
Windsor Rd.	12	E3
Wingate Clo.	21	C4
Wingate Way	21	C4
Woburn Clo.	13	B1
Wolfson College	18	C1
Wolfstan Way	22	D2
Wollaston Rd.	9	C1
Wolsey Way	20	E2
Woodhead Dr.	13	D3
Woodhouse Farm	11	E4
Woodhouse Way	13	E1
Woodlands Pk.	11	A3
Woodlark Rd.	12	D4
Woody Grn.	11	A5
Wooton Way	18	B1
Wordsworth Gro.	8	E2
Wycliffe Rd.	17	A5
Wynford Way	13	B1

Y

Yarrow Rd.	20	G5
York St.	16	E5
York Ter.	16	E5
YMCA	9	B1
Young St.	7	D4
Youth Hostel	19	D2

Z

Zetland Wk.	20	A2
Zoology Museum	8	G5